THE ENGINE
THE HEART OF THE AUTOMOBILE

DEFINITION:

THE HEAT ENGINE IN A VEHICLE IS THE SYSTEM THAT CONVERTS FUEL (HEAT ENERGY) INTO MOTION (MECHANICAL ENERGY).

THE ENGINE'S ROLE IS TO PROVIDE THE NECESSARY AND SUFFICIENT DRIVING ENERGY, SO THAT THE VEHICLE WILL BE ABLE TO MOVE.

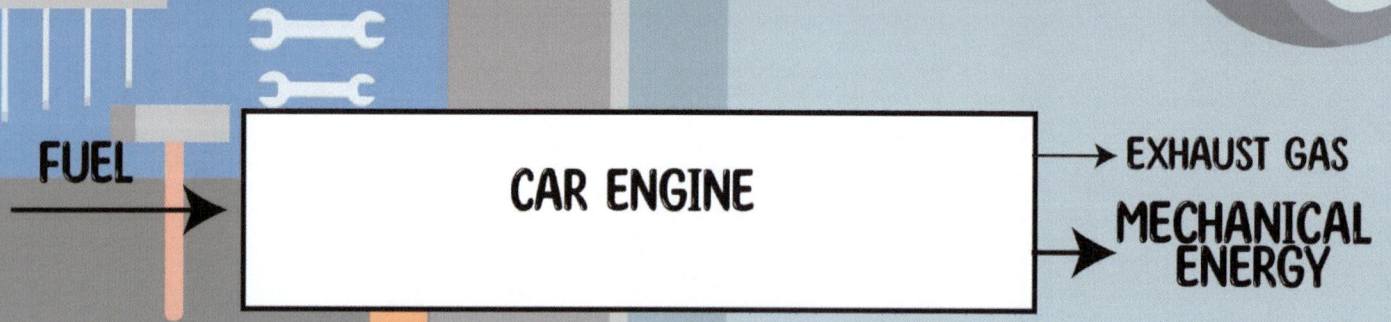

PRINCIPLE:

IT IS CALLED AN INTERNAL COMBUSTION ENGINE (ICE) BECAUSE IT RECEIVES FUEL AND OXYGEN FROM THE AIR) PLUS A SUPPLY OF HEAT CAUSING COMBUSTION INSIDE A CLOSED SYSTEM.

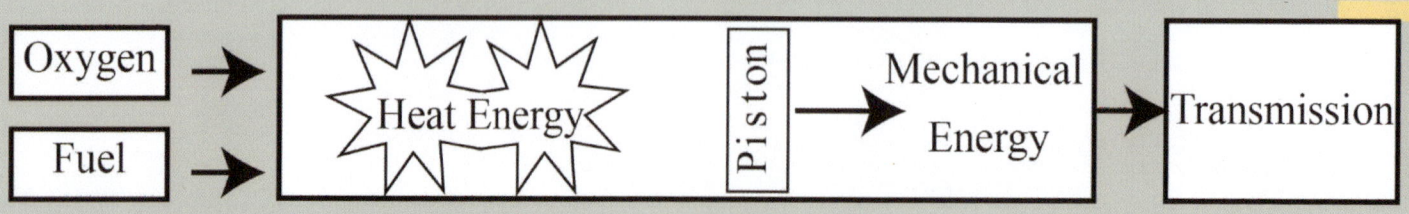

GENERALITIES:

WHAT IS A MOTOR VEHICLE?
A VEHICLE IS DESIGNED TO MOVE IN A GIVEN PATH AND DIRECTION.

THIS MOVEMENT IS ACHIEVED BY MEANS OF AN ENGINE.

THE FUEL ENERGY IS USUALLY USED TO MAKE SUCH MOVEMENT.

AN ENGINE CONVERTS ENERGY FROM THE EXPLOSION OF BURNING GASOLINE INTO MECHANICAL WORK (TORQUE).

THE EXPLOSIN ARE MADE INSIDE THE ENGINE, IN WHAT IS CALLED THE COMBUSTION CHAMBER.

THAT WORK (TORQUE) IS APPLIED TO THE WHEELS TO MAKE THE CAR MOVE.

THE MAIN PARTS OF THE CAR:

THE MOTOR VEHICLE INCLUDES FOUR MAIN ASSEMBLIES:

1. THE MECHANICAL ASSEMBLY COMPOSED OF :
- THE ENGINE, DESIGNED TO PROVIDE THE MECHANICAL ENERGY NECESSARY FOR THE MOVEMENT.

- TRANSMISSION COMPONENTS WHICH TRANSMIT THE MECHANICAL ENERGY TO THE VEHICLE TO MAKE IT MOVE.

- THE OPERATING ELEMENTS (ROAD HOLDING ELEMENTS SUCH AS BRAKES, SUSPENSION AND STEERING) DEDICATED TO DRIVE THE VEHICLE, TO STOP IT AND TO ENSURE ITS SUSPENSION.

2. THE ELECTRICAL SYSTEM THAT CONDUCTS, STORES AND DISTRIBUTES THIS ENERGY NECESSARY TO OPERATE THE ENGINE AND VARIOUS ACCESSORIES.

3. THE CHASSIS, WHOSE ROLE IS TO RECEIVE THE MECHANICAL COMPONENTS (E.G. ENGINE, TRANSMISSION, ETC.) AND TO SUPPORT THE BODYWORK.

4. THE BODYWORK ASSEMBLY WHICH SERVES AS A LIVING SPACE AND SHELTER FOR THE DRIVER AND PASSENGERS, OR POSSIBLY, AS A PLACE FOR VARIOUS GOODS.

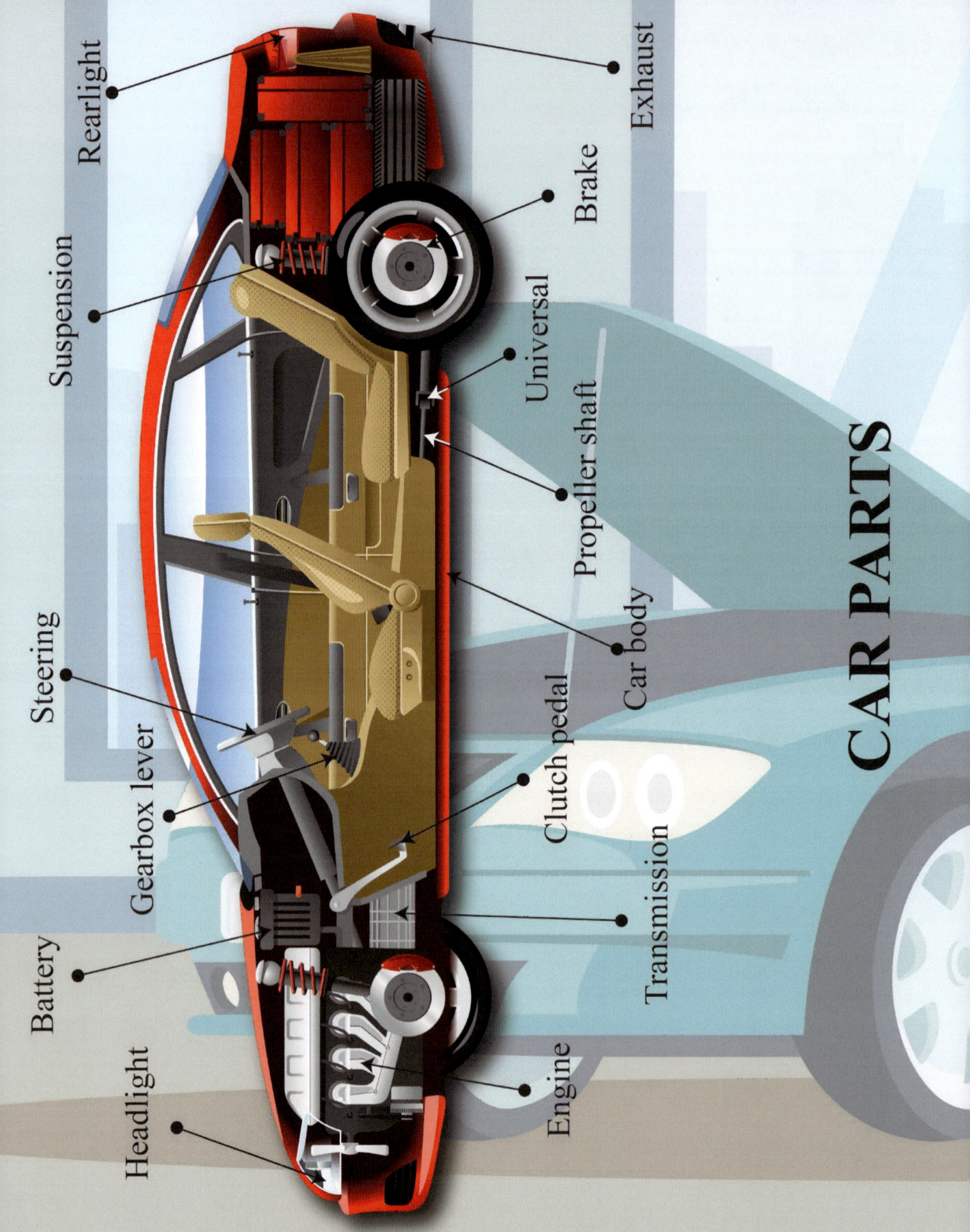

HEAT ENGINES CLASSIFICATION:

THERE ARE TWO MAIN FAMILIES OF ENGINES. THEY ARE CHARACTERIZED BY THE NATURE OF THE FUEL USED:

- THE EXPLOSION ENGINES (GASOLINE).
- COMBUSTION ENGINES (DIESEL).

THE ENGINE COMPONENTS:

THE ENGINE IS A SET OF COMPONENTS, ITSELF COMPOSED OF VARIOUS SUB-ASSEMBLIES.

THE CONSTITUENT PARTS:

CYLINDER HEAD

MOVING PARTS

DISTRIBUTION SYSTEM

CYLINDER BLOCK

THE DIFFERENT PARTS OF THE ENGINE:

WE DISTINGUISH IN AN ENGINE BETWEEN: - FIXED PARTS AND MOVING PARTS.

THE PRINCIPAL FIXED PARTS ARE:
ENGINE HEAD, ENGINE BLOCK AND CRANKCASE.

THE PRINCIPAL MOVING PARTS ARE:
PISTONS, CONNECTING RODS, CRANKSHAFT. CAMSHAFTS. VALVES. AND GEAR TRAIN.

FIXED ELEMENTS:

CYLINDER BLOCK:
IT IS THE MAIN PART OF THE ENGINE. THEREFORE, IT ENSURES SEVERAL ESSENTIAL FUNCTIONS, NAMELY:
- SUPPORTING THE CYLINDER HEAD.
- GUIDING THE PISTONS.
- GUIDING THE CRANKSHAFT.
- CONTAIN THE COOLANT.

FOUR CYLINDER ENGINE.

CYLINDER HEAD:

IT IS PLACED ABOVE THE CYLINDER BLOCK. IT ALSO CONTAINS THE INTAKE AND EXHAUST PORTS.

CYLINDER HEAD.

THE CYLINDER HEAD COMPRISES:
- THE COMBUSTION CHAMBER;
- THE SPARK PLUG (GASOLINE ENGINE) OR INJECTOR (DIESEL ENGINE).
- VALVES.

CRANKCASE:

THE CRANKCASE IS LOCATED UNDER THE CYLINDER BLOCK. IT CONTAINS THE OIL NECESSARY TO LUBRICATE THE MOVING PARTS.

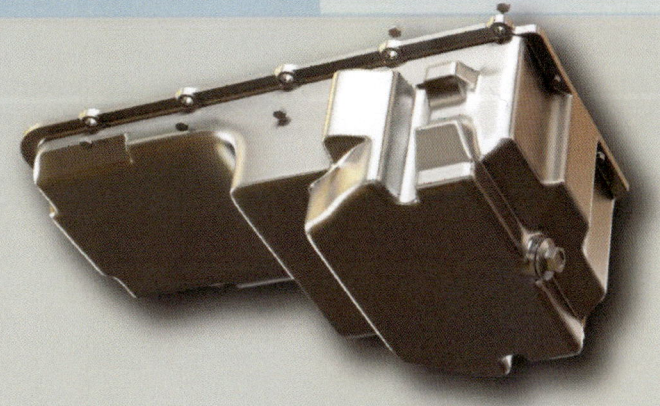
CRANKCASE

THE MOBILE EQUIPMENT :
IT CONSISTS OF :

THE PISTON, CONNECTING ROD, CRANKSHAFT AND FLYWHEEL.

PISTON :

THE CONNECTING ROD :

CRANKSHAFT AND FLYWHEEL :

CRANKSHAFT

FLYWHEEL

THE PISTON, CONNECTING ROD, CRANKSHAFT AND FLYWHEEL ASSEMBLY, FORMING THE MOBILE EQUIPMENT.

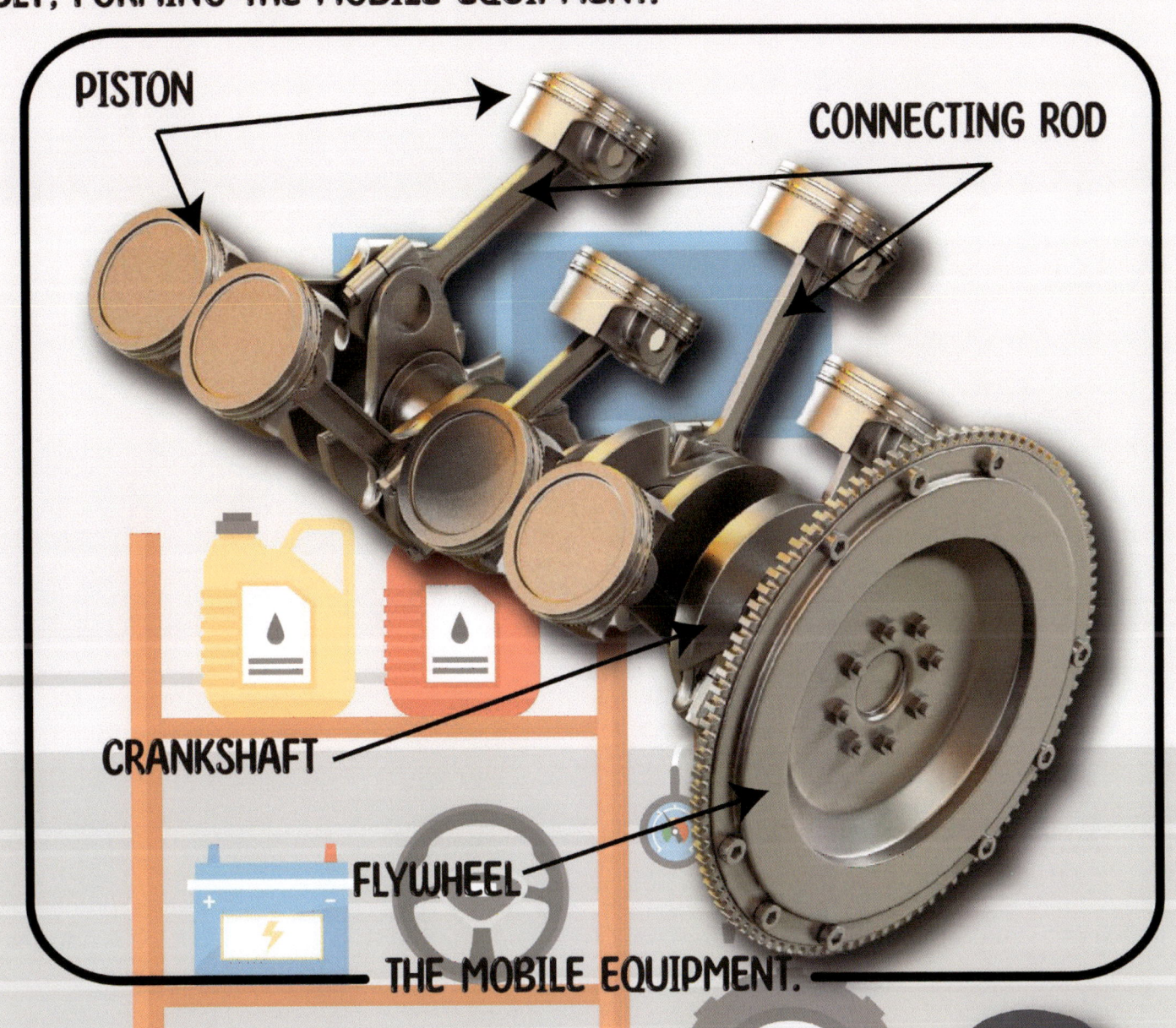

OTHER PART;

VALVE; PERMITTING THE ENTRY AND EXIT OF GASES, AND ENSURING THE SEALING WHEN CLOSING.

GASOLINE ENGINE

FIRST STROKE, INTAKE:

GASOLINE MOVES THROUGHT THE FUEL SYSTEM AND INTO FUEL INJECTORS.

THE INTAKE VALVE ALLOWS A MIX OF AIR AND FUEL INTO THE CYLINDER.

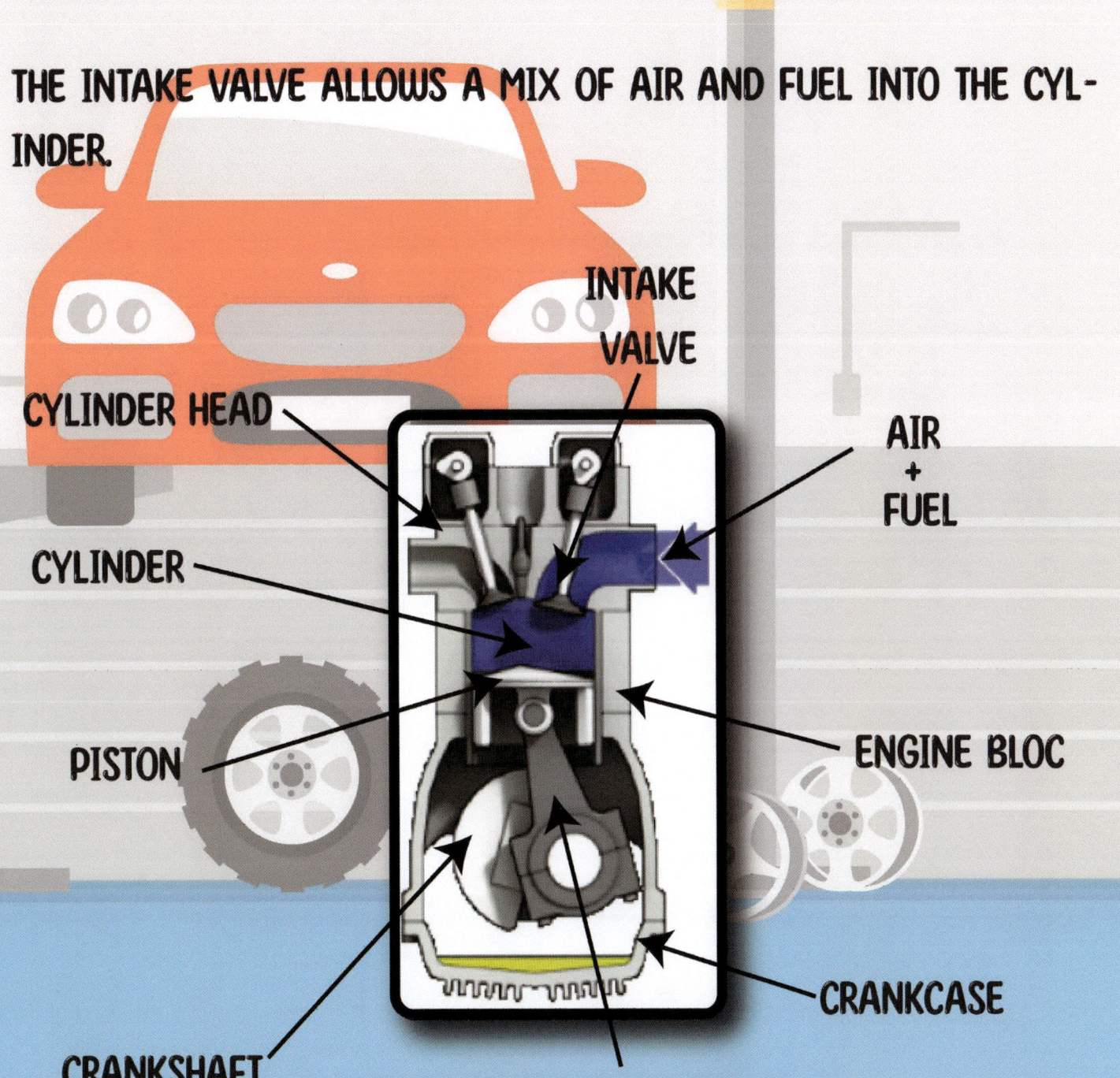

- INTAKE VALVE
- AIR + FUEL
- CYLINDER HEAD
- CYLINDER
- ENGINE BLOC
- PISTON
- CRANKCASE
- CRANKSHAFT
- CONNECTING ROD

SECOND STROKE, COMPRESSION.
THE BOTH VALVES ARE CLOSED.

THE FUEL MIXTURE (AIR/GASOLINE) IS COMPRESSED BY THE PISTON.

AT THE END OF THE COMPRESSION, THE SPARK CREATES COMBUSTION.

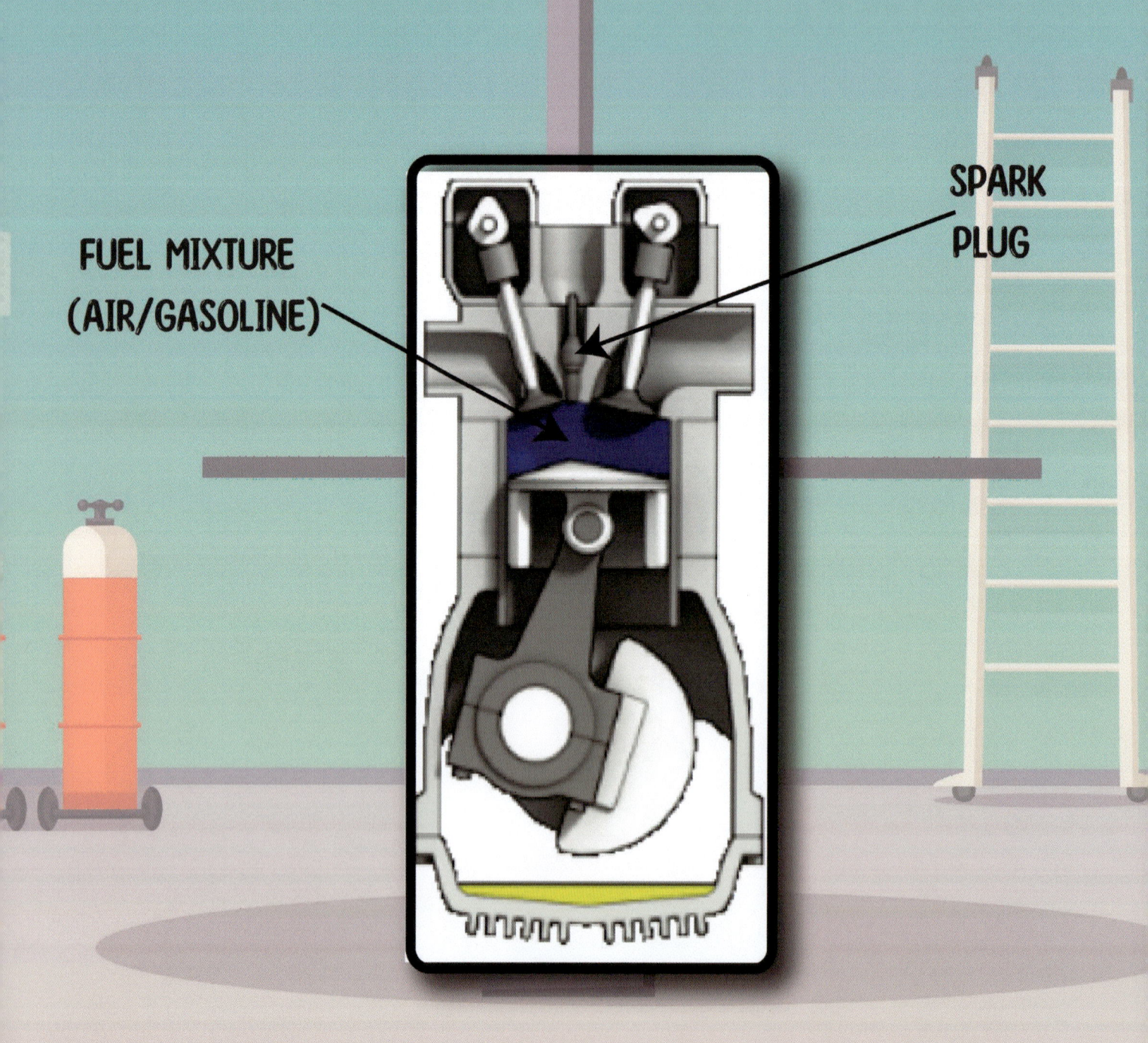

FUEL MIXTURE (AIR/GASOLINE)

SPARK PLUG

THIRD STROKE: POWER

THE INLET AND EXHAUST VALVES ARE CLOSED.

WHEN THE PISTON HAS RISEN, THE SPARK PLUG IGNITES THE MIXTURE, CAUSING AN **EXPLOSION.**

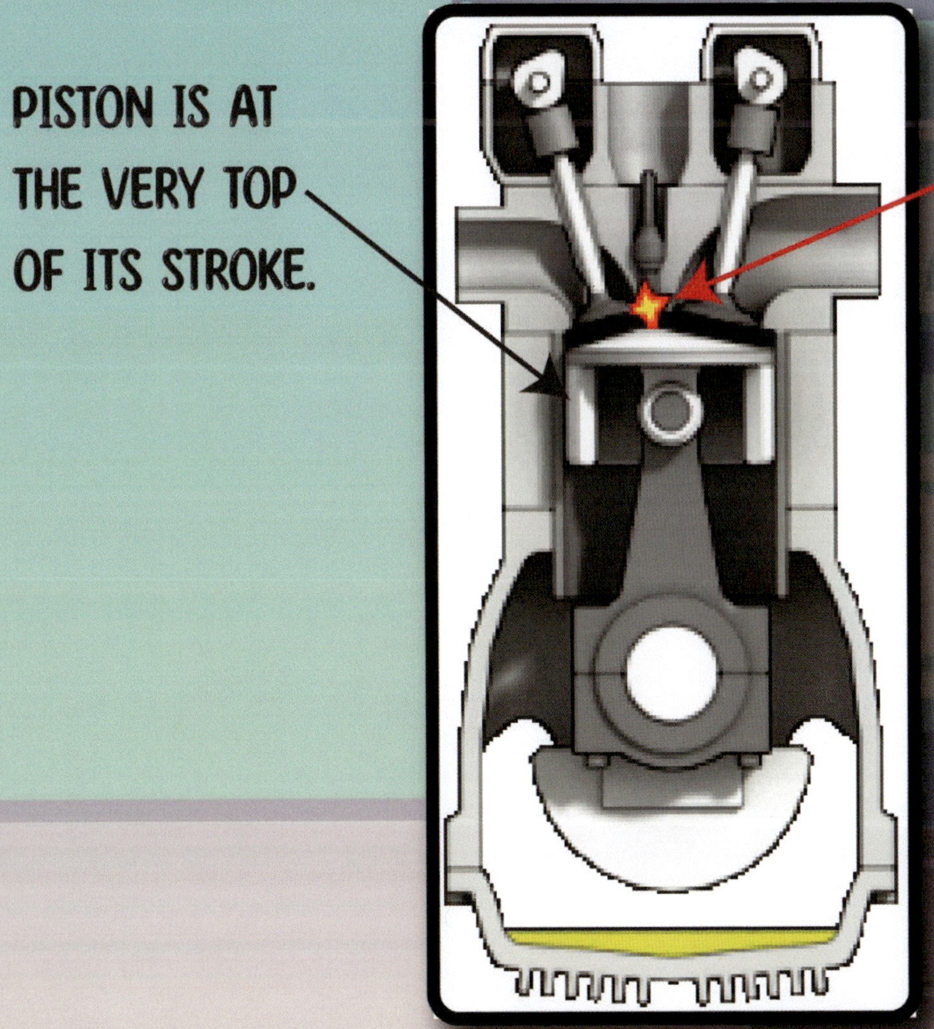

PISTON IS AT THE VERY TOP OF ITS STROKE.

SPARK

FOURTH STROKE, EXHAUST:

THE EXHAUST VALVE IS OPEN, THE INTAKE VALVE CLOSED.

THE EXHAUST VALVE ALLOWS THE BURNT GASES TO ESCAPE.

EXHAUST VALVE

BURNT GASES

DIESEL ENGINE

FIRST STROKE, INTAKE:

THE INTAKE VALVE IS OPEN, THE EXHAUST VALVE IS CLOSED.

THE INTAKE VALVE ALLOWS THE AIR INTO THE CYLINDER.

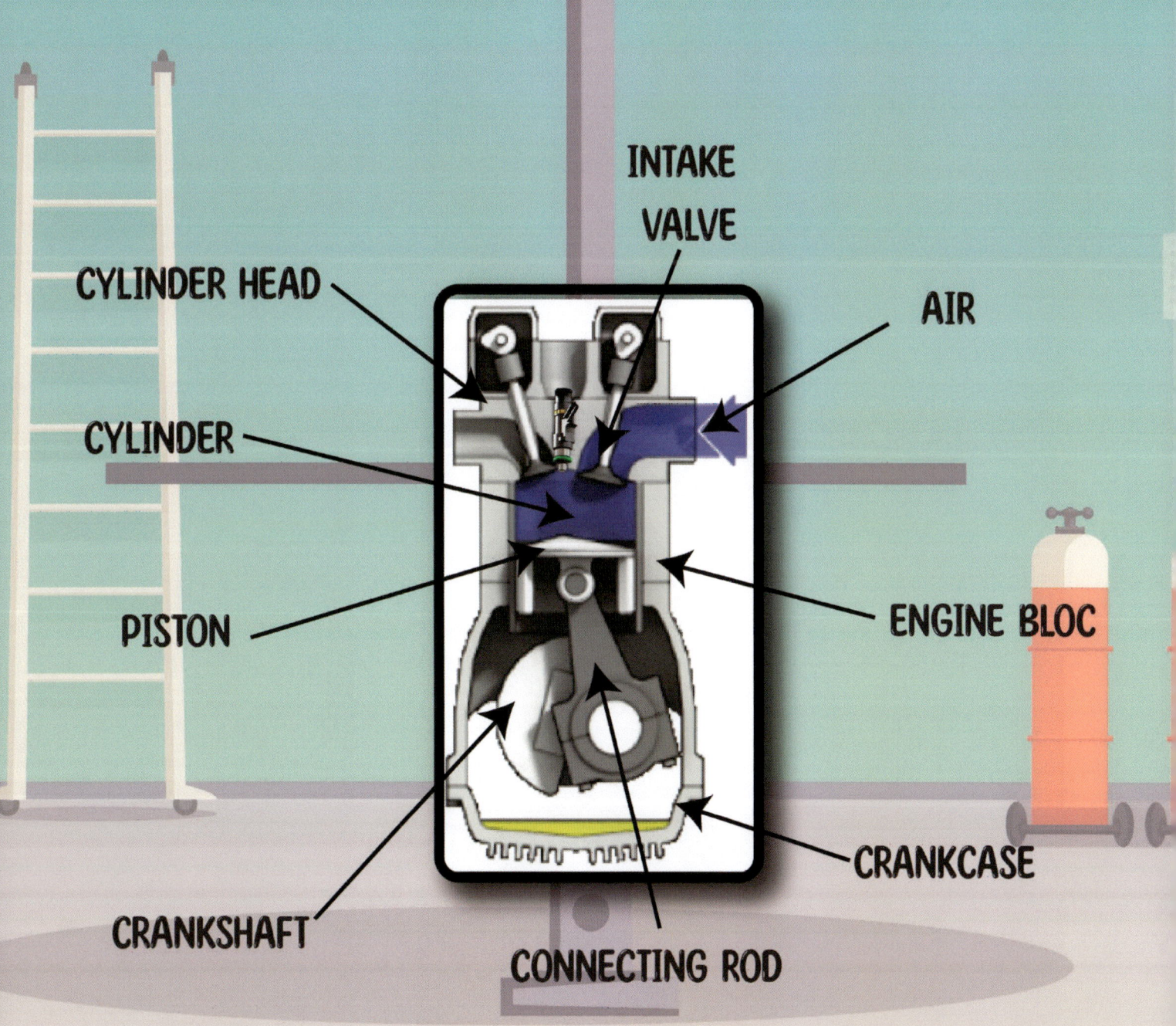

- INTAKE VALVE
- AIR
- CYLINDER HEAD
- CYLINDER
- ENGINE BLOC
- PISTON
- CRANKCASE
- CRANKSHAFT
- CONNECTING ROD

SECOND STROKE, COMPRESSION:

THE BOTH VALVES ARE CLOSED.

THE AIR IS COMPRESSED BY THE PISTON.

COMPRESSION RAISES THE TEMPERATURE OF THE AIR.

AT THE END OF THE COMPRESSION, THE FUEL IS INJECTED THROUGH THE INJECTOR INTO THE COMBUSTION CHAMBER.

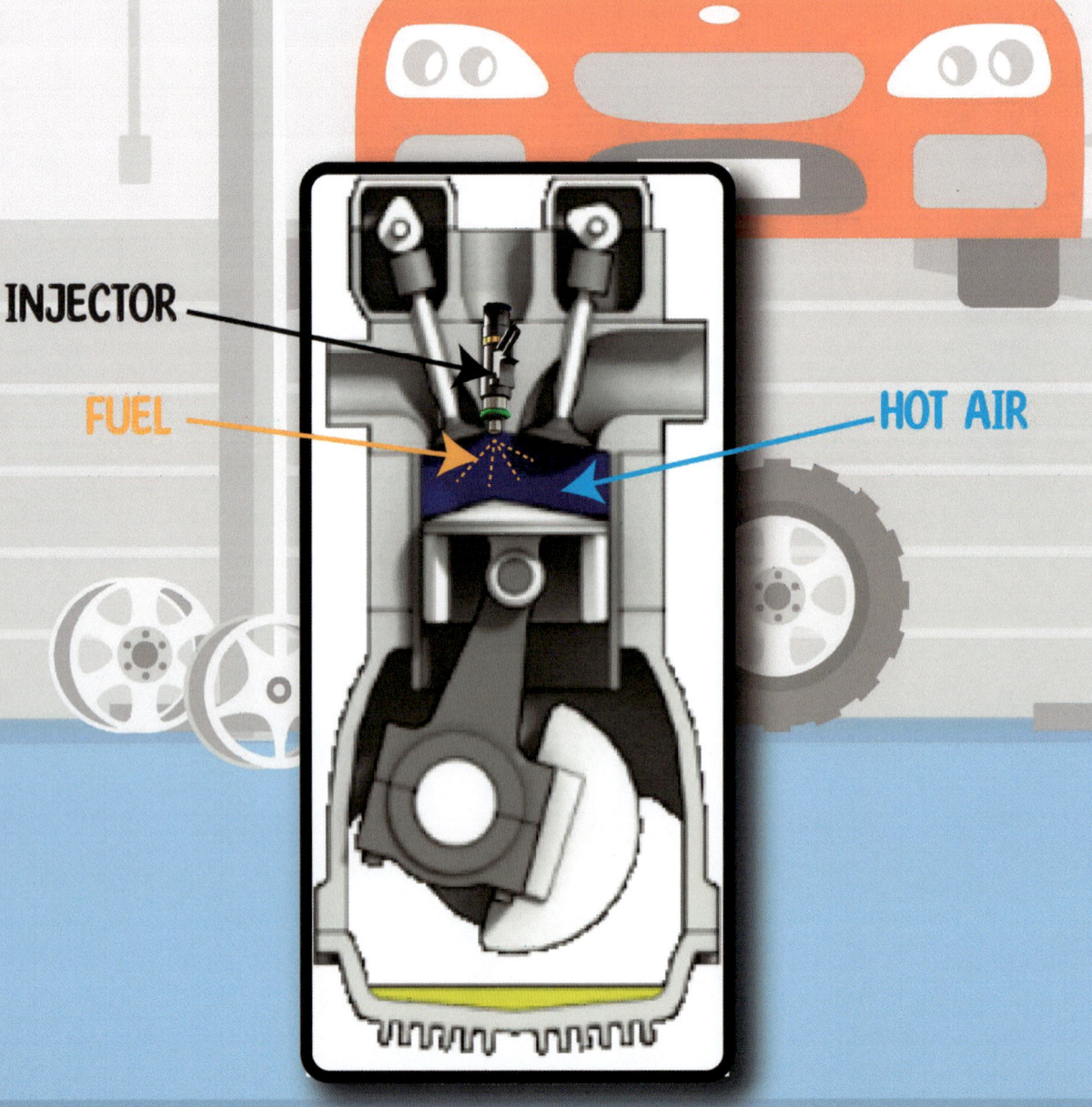

THIRD STROKE: POWER

THE INLET AND EXHAUST VALVES ARE CLOSED.

THE FUEL IGNITES SPONTANEOUSLY ON CONTACT WITH THE HOT AIR, CAUSING AN **EXPLOSION**.

FOURTH STROKE, EXHAUST:

THE EXHAUST VALVE IS OPEN, THE INTAKE VALVE CLOSED.

THE EXHAUST VALVE ALLOWS THE BURNT GASES TO ESCAPE.

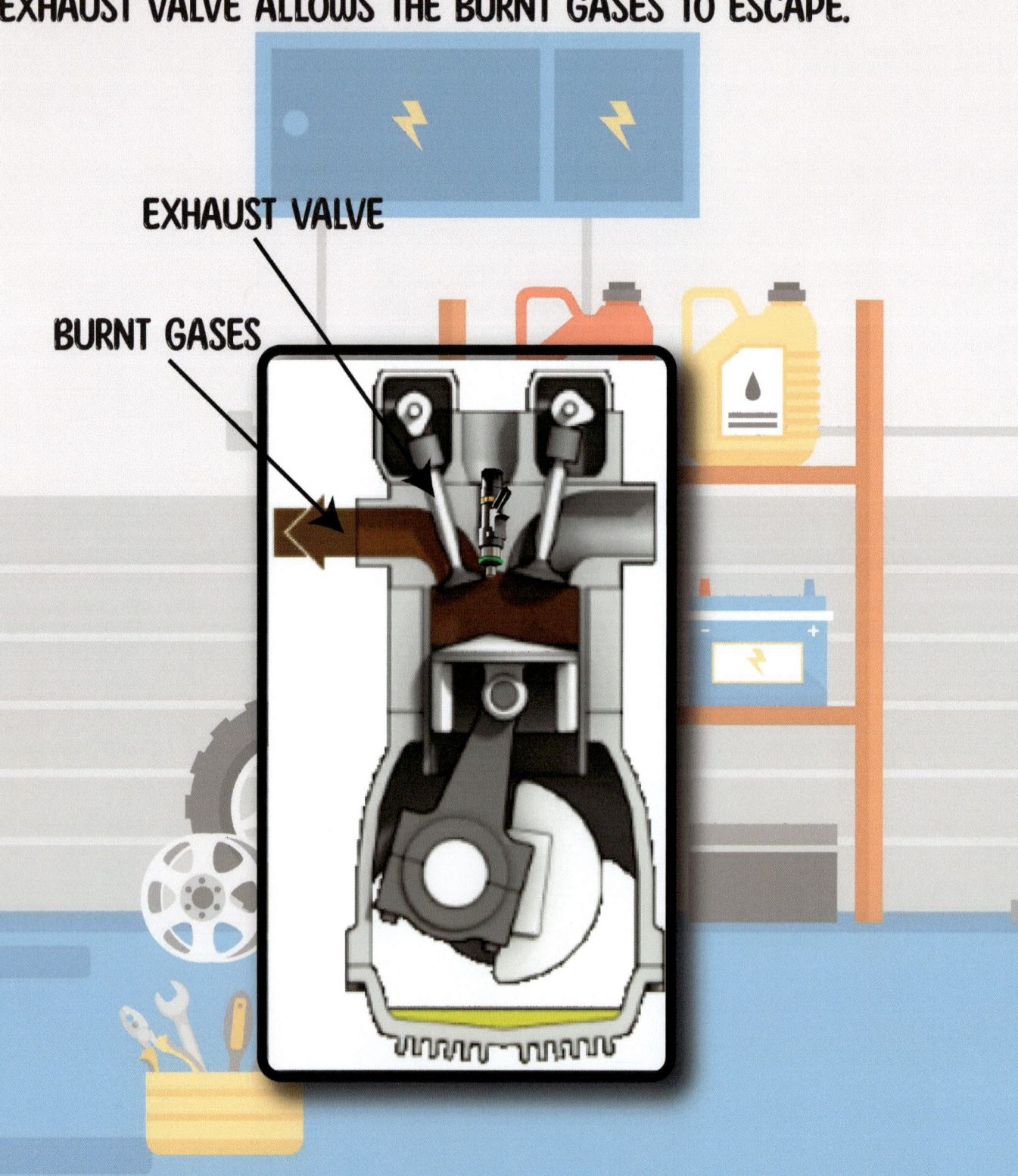

YOU GET HOW POWER IS GENERATED INSIDE THE CYLINDER, NOW

HOW CAR CONVERT THAT COMBUSTION TO MOTION?

THE MOVEMENT OF THE PISTONS DRIVES THE CRANK SHAFT UP AND DOWN.

THE SPINNING CRANKSHAFT TURNS THE FLYWHEEL.

THE FLYWHEEL IS CONNECTED TO THE TRANSMISSION.

THE TRANSMISSION THEN CONNECTS TO THE DRIVE THE WHEELS.

THE TURNING WHEELS IN TURN MOVE THE CAR.

TRANMISSION

THE TRANSMISSION IS THE SET OF ELEMENTS THAT TRANSMIT THE MOVEMENT OF THE ENGINE TO THE DRIVE WHEELS.

ITS PURPOSE IS TO TRANSMIT AND VARY THE ROTATION SPEED OF THE ENGINE TO THE DRIVE WHEELS.

CONSTITUENT SUB-ASSEMBLIES:
1. THE CLUTCH.
2. THE GEARBOX.
3. THE DIFFERENTIAL.

1- THE CLUTCH:
THE CLUTCH SYSTEM PARTICIPATES IN THE TRANSMISSION OF POWER FROM THE ENGINE TO THE DRIVE WHEELS.

2- THE GEARBOX
THE SPEED OF AN INTERNAL COMBUSTION ENGINE INCLUDES A MINIMUM AND A MAXIMUM VALUE.
WHATEVER THE TRAFFIC CONDITIONS, THE VEHICLE MUST BE DRIVEN AT THE RIGHT SPEED FOR THE ENGINE. THIS IS MADE POSSIBLE BY THE GEARBOX.

3- THE DRIVING AXLE:

LET'S OBSERVE A MOTOR VEHICLE TAKING A TURN;
WE NOTICE THAT THE OUTER WHEELS TRAVEL A GREATER DISTANCE
THAN THE INNER WHEELS, SO THEY TURN AT DIFFERENT SPEEDS.

THE USE OF A DIFFERENTIAL, ENABLES THE TWO DRIVING WHEELS TO
POSSIBLY TURN AT, DIFFERENT SPEEDS.

- ENGINE
- GEAR BOX
- DIFFERENTIAL

ENGINE LUBRICATION

AN AUTOMOBILE HAS A VERY LARGE NUMBER OF PARTS IN MOTION RELATIVE TO EACH OTHER.

REMINDERS :

WHEN TWO BODIES SLIDE ON EACH OTHER, A PHENOMENON OF FRICTION OCCURS.

THE FRICTION CAN BE:
- USEFUL (CASE OF BRAKING);
- HARMFUL (PRODUCES A RISE IN TEMPERATURE).

THE LUBRICATION, ON A CAR, PERMIT:
- REDUCING FRICTION BETWEEN THE PARTS IN CONTACT;
- AVOIDING THE WEAR OF THE MOBILE PARTS;
- REDUCING THE NOISE OF VARIOUS MECHANISMS.

AN ENGINE HAS SEVERAL POINTS TO BE LUBRICATED:
- CYLINDERS;
- CRANKSHAFT;
- CONNECTING ROD ...

COMPONENTS OF THE PRESSURE

THE PRESSURE LUBRICATION SYSTEM CONSISTS OF AN OIL PUMP, FILTER, RESERVOIR.

THE RESERVOIR: THE LUBRICATING OIL IS CONTAINED IN THE ENGINE CRANKCASE.

THE OIL PUMP: IT DRAWS OIL FROM THE RESERVOIR AND DELIVERS IT TO THE COMPONENTS TO BE LUBRICATED.

THE FILTER: REMOVE IMPURITIES SUSPENDED IN THE OIL.

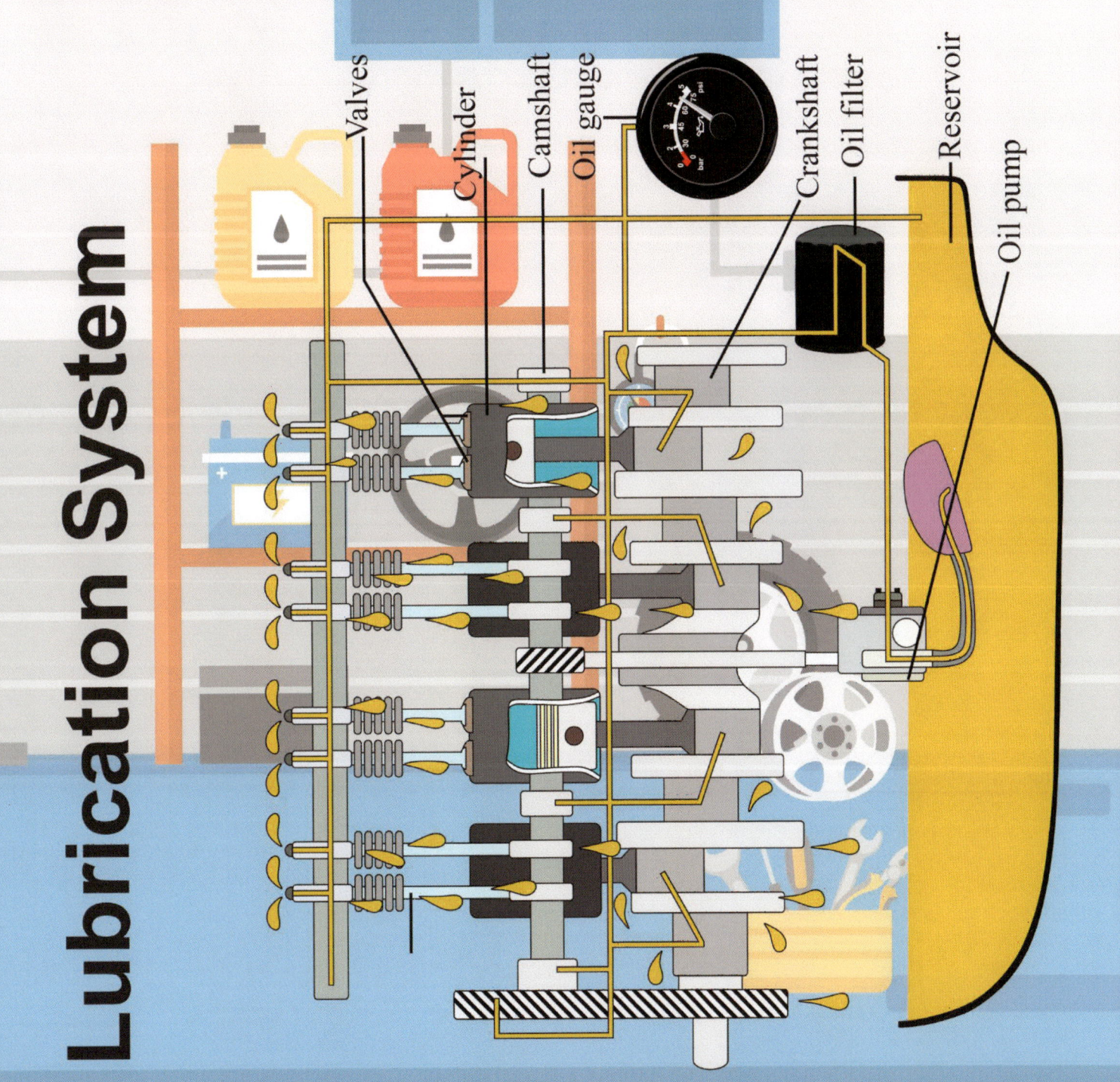

ENGINE COOLING

IN AN ENGINE, THE HEAT RESULTING FROM THE COMBUSTION IS VERY IMPORTANT.

IT IS NECESSARY TO EVACUATE IT. OTHERWISE, THE ENGINE WILL DETERIORATE VERY QUICKLY.

IT RESULTS ESSENTIALLY FROM :
- THE COMBUSTION.
- FRICTION OF THE ENGINE'S MOVING PARTS.

IT IS IMPORTANT TO KEEP THE OPERATING TEMPERATURE BETWEEN 80 AND 110 °C.

TO AVOID THIS, THE ENGINE IS EQUIPPED WITH A COOLING SYSTEM SUPPOSED TO BE VERY EFFICIENT.

FLUID COOLING:
THIS IS THE MOST COMMONLY USED COOLING SYSTEM.

WATER IS THE COOLING FLUID A PUMP DRAWS WATER FROM THE TANK AND PUMPS IT TO THE RADIATOR.

IN FACT, THE WATER CIRCULATING THROUGH THE THE RADIATOR IS COOLED BY AIR.

THE WATER PUMP:

INCREASES THE SPEED OF THE COOLANT.

WATER PUMP

RADIATOR:

THE RADIATOR IS LOCATED AT THE FRONT OF THE VEHICLE. THE RADIATOR CONSISTS OF A NETWORK OF THIN TUBES THAT INCREASES THE AIR/WATER CONTACT SURFACE.

FAN:

ITS PURPOSE IS TO SUPPLY SUFFICIENT COOLING AIR WHEN THE AIRFLOW RESULTED BY THE MOVEMENT OF THE VEHICLE IS INSUFFICIENT TO COOL THE WATER.

THE COOLANT:

IT IS THE TRANSPORT AGENT.

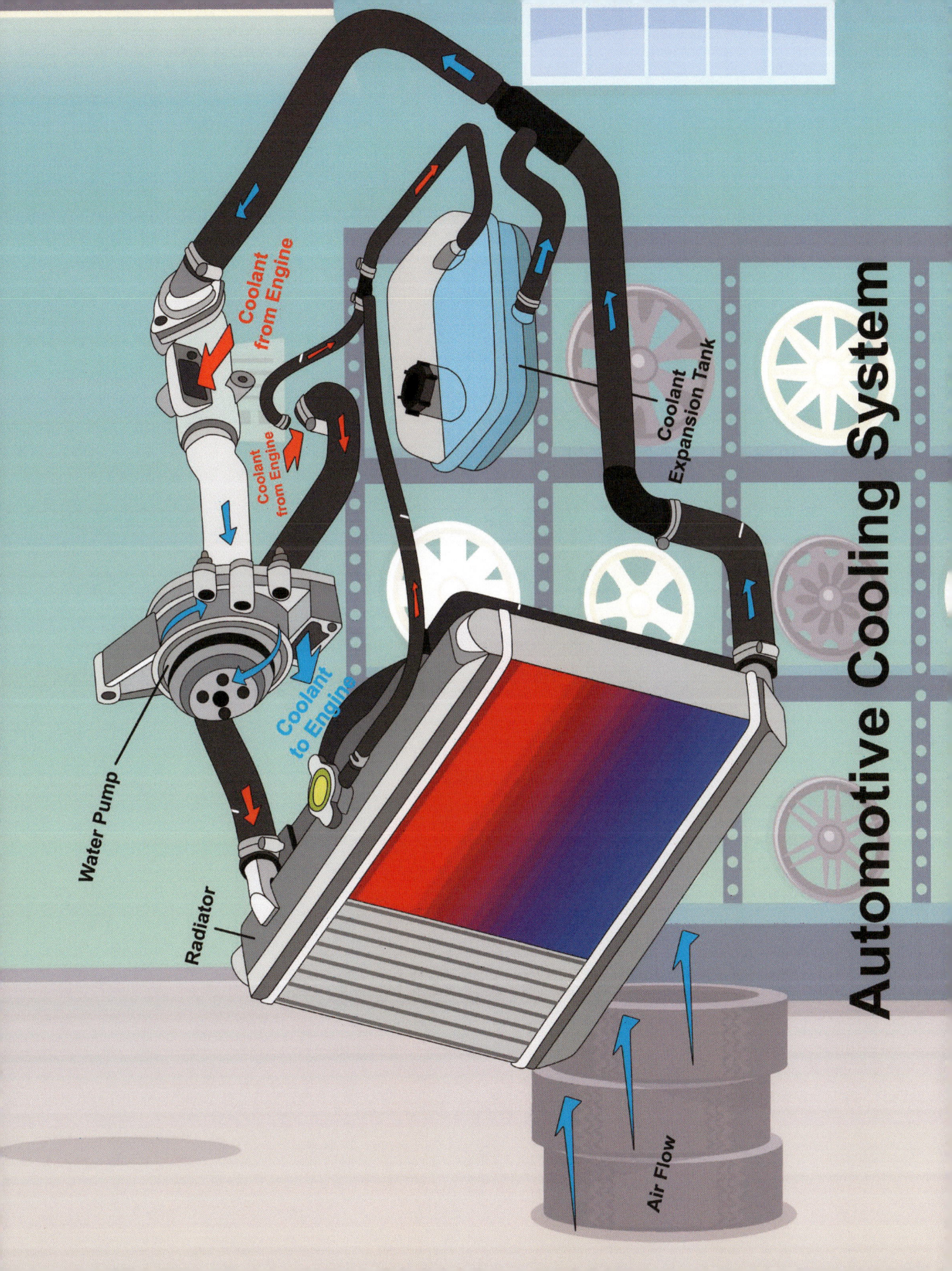

We will be pleased to read your feedback.
Thankyou.

Interior background designed by:

NACreative / Freepik;

pikisuperstar / Freepik.

Cover Designed by:

Macrovector / Freepik;

Vectorpocket / Freepik;

Graphiqastock / Freepik;

Brgfx / Freepik.

Printed in Great Britain
by Amazon